PRED

The
Theatre

BENEDICT NIGHTINGALE

PHŒNIX

A PHOENIX PAPERBACK

First published in Great Britain in 1998 by
Phoenix, a division of the Orion Publishing Group Ltd
Orion House
5 Upper Saint Martin's Lane
London, WC2H 9EA

A CIP catalogue record for this book is available
from the British Library.

ISBN 0 297 81957 7

Typeset by SetSystems Ltd, Saffron Walden
Set in 9/11 Stone Serif
Printed in Great Britain by
Clays Ltd, St Ives plc

Acknowledgements

I would like to thank those with whom I had helpful conversations while I was researching this book, including Anna Stapleton, Kate Devey, Sue Rose, Thelma Holt, Mark Fisher, Edward Snape, David Edgar, Stephen Daldry, Nicholas Barter, Philip Hedley, Nick Salmon and Peter Roberts.

Contents

Chapter 1
Pangloss Speaks

Back in 1897 a critic called Augustin Filon cast a cool Gallic eye over the British theatre. Who, he asked in his *The English Stage*, would join Pinero, Jones and Grundy as the important dramatists of tomorrow? G. R. Sims, probably. Perhaps Louis N. Parker, Malcolm Watson, Haddon Chambers and J. M. Barrie. Moreover, those young Turks would soon be rid of a censor who had recently objected to the line 'he plays the violin like an angel' on the grounds of its blasphemy and even banned the word 'thigh'. The Lord Chamberlain's power over the theatre would disappear, declared Filon, though so gradually nobody would notice when the *coup de grâce* came.

Prophets, be warned. Seventy years later the Lord Chamberlain was requiring producers of plays by (respectively) Osborne and Buchner to substitute 'muffin' for 'crumpet' and 'the Devil!' for 'Jesus!'. Not until 1968 did the old gentleman receive a death-blow that, far from passing unnoticed, was celebrated by the sensationalism of *Oh, Calcutta!*. Again, Grundy and even Jones have long been rotting in the oubliette to which Sims, Parker and Watson were consigned just after *The English Stage* appeared. And if Filon registered Barrie, he was unaware of the Shaw who had already enjoyed West End success with *Arms and the Man*.

Yet Filon did foresee the eventual acceptance and influence of the great Ibsen. Indeed, he prophesied that British dramatists would share the 'labour of creating society afresh' and might produce plays that faced up to the threat of a 'terrible To-morrow'. Thus the flowering of socially purposeful drama in the Edwardian age, with Shaw, Granville Barker and Galsworthy at the roots, wouldn't have surprised Filon. He could, however, hardly have imagined

1

the horrors of the To-morrow that was to impoverish the theatrical garden until the mid-1950s.

But then could there be a more spectacular demonstration of the limitations of prediction than the First World War? All art is directly and indirectly shaped by shifts in society, and that most public of forms, the drama, strongly so. Would even *Waiting for Godot* and *The Birthday Party* be the plays they are if Nazism hadn't impelled Samuel Beckett to join the French resistance and terrified Harold Pinter, a Jewish boy in the East End of London, with bombs and distantly glimpsed atrocities? Theatrical prophesy is therefore doubly, trebly difficult, for playwrights are reacting to events they can't control or foresee, and the most original will do so in unexpected ways. The unpredictable are unpredictably shaped by the unpredictable.

How many British pundits in 1978 foresaw the collapse of socialism? And if the writer of a book like this had spotted the trends, how would he have expected dramatists to react? Given the radical convictions many had paraded when less uncongenial figures than Margaret Thatcher held power, protest should have resounded round our stages. Yet that didn't happen. True, Caryl Churchill wrote *Top Girls* and *Serious Money* and Doug Lucie *Fashion*; but comparably scathing attacks on the brutalisation of Britain seldom emerged. Writers whose worst nightmares had arrived with Mrs Thatcher seemed mesmerized, like furry animals faced with a cobra. What should have been a blazing decade for new drama was incongruously quiet.

So how will British playwrights react to a fascist regime in Russia, to terrorists with nuclear weapons, to China's growing power, to a centralized Europe under German hegemony, to chasms between the privileged and an embittered underclass at home, to global warming and rising seas, or whatever else happens in the century ahead? And who will the 'British' be anyway? Who will sit in the theatres, if they still exist, and savour the dramatic fallout?

In 1897 Filon summed up the British as 'a race of heroes who are also buccaneers, a race of poets and shopkeepers, a race fearless of death and devoted to money, calculating but passionate, capable of the charges of Balaclava and the deal in the Suez shares'. A century later we're more sceptical and cynical even about our shopkeeping abilities. Yet educational, social and economic change have created a far larger, broader audience for the drama than Filon envisaged. When I go to Shaftesbury Avenue I don't see men in white ties, and even on the fringe I seldom feel I'm in an earnest intellectual ghetto, like the Independent Theatre on an Ibsen evening.

True, surveys suggest that, except when musicals are showing, classes A and B are much more likely to visit the theatre than classes C and D. The old divides between stalls and balcony, or between the audiences for Pinero and those for music hall, have changed less than we like to think. I see different audiences at *Grease* or Cliff Richard's *Heathcliff* from those I see at the National, and, with top tickets there now £24 or more, I see generally older people at the National than at the Bush or my local cinema. Yet roughly twenty-five million visits were annually made to English theatres in the mid-1990s, four million of them by foreign visitors.

Though a total of twenty-five million visits doesn't mean that twenty-five million different people were going to the theatre, still less that there is a multi-million audience for Strindberg and Stoppard, the scattershot accusations of elitism sometimes directed at the theatre are misplaced. The million-plus people who by late 1997 had seen Stephen Daldry's revival of J. B. Priestley's *An Inspector Calls* in London cannot all have been university graduates. There's a big, varied audience out there and, admittedly depending on what happens to our education system and our economy, it will get bigger and more varied. That's a cause for optimism, and there are others. We have the actors, the directors, maybe even the writers to reanimate the theatre, ensure its cultural centrality, and conceivably

3

justify its reputation, not solely held in Britain itself, as the best in the world.

Does this sound Panglossian? Perhaps. Those artists and their descendants can't thrive without the right conditions. I am, I suppose, a Pangloss uneasily aware that beneath the rich-looking soil there are faults that could erupt into the theatre's own Lisbon earthquake. To put it another way, Sod's Law won't be suspended just because it's 2010, 2020 or 2050 AD.

Chapter 2
Why the Theatre Will Matter

My main reason for optimism is not the talent the theatre can boast nor the occasional genius it may produce. It is rather that the theatre will soon be wanted, needed, as never before. The performing arts will be required to satisfy an appetite as compelling as any in their 2,500-year-old history.

This may seem a perverse view. When 300 television channels are beaming down, won't our living rooms be theatres enough? When we can slip a sliver of fabric into the wall, speak a number, and call up anything on a space as large and multi-dimensional as we wish, won't the most voracious appetite for entertainment and the arts be satisfied? Quite the contrary. However vast the impact of new technology on the world's leisure patterns, it is still good news for the live theatre.

That's not merely because it's hard to adapt any but the most realistic drama to the screen. Again, it has little to do with the quality of the work on offer. Even if dramatists as great as Chekhov are writing scripts for the digital era, and four generations of the Redgrave dynasty performing them, something crucial will be missing. Call it human contact, risk or fallibility. It is what makes theatre theatre. It is also what makes theatre necessary.

True, one can imagine a future in which people retreat into their dens, swallow tranquillizers along with robot-provided food, bury themselves in virtual-reality apparatus, and disappear into a fantasy-world of fun and factitious relationships. But the Policy Studies Institute's 'Cultural Trends' suggest an opposite scenario. Its figures report an increase in the percentage of the population visiting the theatre between 1985 and 1995, and a decrease in the amount of television watched. People yearn to be active and (at times) communal, not passive and desolately surfing dreamland. However brilliantly they let us fake participation, the new media prohibit the real thing.

For the critic George Steiner, this electronic revolution is 'much more consequential than Gutenberg. We can', he declared in 1996, 'scarcely calculate the mutations in our experience of texts, music and art in the new world of the CD-ROM, of virtual reality, of cyberspace and the internet.' Add cable, and 'the options for enjoyment will be almost unlimited'. Yet these changes will 'put a fresh premium on physical immediacy'.

Surely that's a justified claim. The most remarkable performances conjured up by the most sophisticated machines are set, fixed, happening in the past, not the present. The creativity is over. We can fast-forward and rewind, applaud and boo, and still the same faces wear the same expressions, the identical voices emit the identical intonations. We receive, but we do not give, still less change anything. It has been observed that people watching film or TV tend to lean back, people in a theatre to lean forward. That body-language tells a truth. However hard it may strive to be trivial, the theatre cannot shed the civic and religious importance it possessed at its dawning. Actors involve us here and now in debates, however superficial, and in rituals, however debased.

If every performance of a film is the same, the opposite is true of a play. Indeed, there's no such thing as a play, given the myriad tilts that texts acquire as performers react to audiences whose composition changes nightly and whose moods shift from moment to moment. We don't need to shout and throw tomatoes, as audiences once did. Positive, negative, whatever, our emotions cross the footlights. There is always give-and-take. We are part of a circle, a spiral, or a psychic ball-game, in which feeling endlessly moves between actors and spectators, changing both parties as it goes. Spectators are always players.

Most theatregoers will have their own exhilarating memories. Myself, I recall the transcendent ferocity of Barbara

Jefford's Phèdre in a Salford theatre so dilapidated that the urinals were heard loudly flushing every five minutes. I remember the scene in a New York production of Arthur Miller's *Death of a Salesman* when Dustin Hoffman's Willy Loman cradled John Malkovich's Biff in a display of paternal tenderness of frightening intimacy. I recall Eileen Atkins, in Tennessee Williams's *Night of the Iguana* at the National, gravely describing a furtive erotic encounter in a boat off Singapore.

It's hard to define what happened on those occasions. Maybe Brian Friel found the right analogue in *Faith Healer*, a play about a shaman capable of performing sporadic wonders, but never sure when they would occur. But in each of those theatres stage and auditorium seemed to be one. Audiences and performers were generating and sharing feelings at once profound, elusive and, it seemed, unique. I daresay nothing remarkable happened the next night at the same moments, for such communions cannot be planned or easily repeated. But it is that unpredictable magic which raises the theatre to levels closed to the mechanical media. Could Jefford, Atkins, Hoffman or Malkovich have achieved what they did on film, television or CD-ROM, even after a thousand takes? Of course not.

Chapter 3
Theatre Spaces for the Future

But where and how will the creative rapport we crave emerge? The subjects this question raises include drama, acting, directing, design, and, most obviously, architecture. What sort of space will best serve a theatre which wishes effectively to engage, involve, excite, alarm, debate, challenge, move, tickle and/or delight audiences consciously or unconsciously resisting overdoses of canned culture and computerized fun?

Put like that, the question answers itself. Small, intimate and informal is right. Yet I can't forget that all three performances I mentioned a moment ago occurred on apparently unsuitable stages: a big Broadway theatre, the cinema-like Lyttelton, and a conventional playhouse given up for dead by everyone except the occasional toilet-cleaner. Theatrical magic can transcend any obstacle, including the proscenium arches that have divided actors and audiences for over three centuries.

Nevertheless, the reaction against both proscenium arches and large playhouses for anything but stylized plays and operatic musicals has long been under way. A 'theatre' in the 1990s may be an attic, a basement, a segment of street, or anywhere two or three come to perform and six or seven to watch.

Myself, I visit a bewildering variety of spaces: a vast exhibition hall in Birmingham for a reconstruction of Aeschylus' *Danaïdes*; a long, narrow armoury in Dublin's Phoenix Park for Fiona Shaw's performance of Eliot's *Four Quartets*; a theatre-in-the-round in a converted Scarborough cinema; a swimming-pool in Edinburgh for a Ukrainian version of *Othello* set mostly in the water. I frequent tiny rooms above pubs; theatres with open stages, like those at Chichester or Nottingham; and Stratford's Swan, which is indebted to Shakespeare's Globe. But most often I go to playhouses constructed along traditional lines: the Royal Shakespeare Theatre at Stratford, the Lyttelton in London, many regional theatres and virtually all those in the West End and on Broadway.

Ideally each play should dictate the nature of the space in which it is performed, and in some studio theatres this does happen. The well of the National's Cottesloe, for instance, can mutate into several different configurations, or be stripped bare for a 'promenade performance' such as a superb production of medieval mysteries in which spectators stood inches from a graphically crucified Christ. Yet this question will present itself increasingly urgently in the next millennium: is the geography of our stages and our auditoria right for our directors and playwrights?

Nobody handles a large stage better than Trevor Nunn – witness his co-productions with John Caird of *Nicholas Nickleby* and *Les Misérables* – but he has declared that Shakespeare acquires most eloquence and impact in smallish theatres: 'We've become accustomed to the idea of his being performed in 19th-century theatres so large the actor has to declaim. But does the use of highly poetic language mean the plays are rhetorical exercises? I don't think so. I believe many more than we think are damaged by the idea that there's a rhetorical music to them rather than a dialectical precision.'

Nunn proceeded to make his point with fine productions of *Measure for Measure* and *Timon of Athens*. And as head of the National, he will find that many of the most gifted younger directors hold similar views. It will be easier to attract the likes of Katie Mitchell and Deborah Warner to the 260-seat Cottesloe than to the much larger Lyttelton and Olivier. Stephen Daldry, too, believes that small, intimate spaces are the way of the future; and his views have special weight because he has enjoyed great success on large stages. If a play on a broad social theme will gain from extravagantly expressionistic treatment – as with his revivals of Priestley's *An Inspector Calls* and Sophie Treadwell's *Machinal* at the National – he can cope with it. Yet he sees and supports a general trend towards small theatres.

In the larger conventional theatres, he feels, audiences are spectators merely, but in small ones they are unwittingly transformed into participants: 'The spaces ask you to enter an imaginative world, not passively to view it.' So keen was he to substitute immediacy and excitement for distance and detachment that he temporarily reconstructed the innards of the Royal Court, whose artistic director he was until late 1997. Audiences for his revival of Arnold Wesker's *Kitchen* found a shimmering array of stoves and steel cupboards where the stalls had been.

But creative demolition is seldom possible and questionably desirable. Didn't Brecht build a theory round the idea that distance and detachment forced audiences to resist dramatic illusion and internally debate the issues he raised? Yes, but he was thinking less of size than of style. For what it's worth, he would have preferred a buttonholing immediacy than remote dialectics in some theatrical cavern, especially if it came with boxes, circles, gilded angels and other traditional accoutrements.

Again, how can we lose the often beautiful theatres we have inherited? If we wanted to do so, we probably couldn't, for Shaftesbury Avenue and even Broadway enjoy a high degree of environmental protection. Though New York lost two playhouses to the developers in the early 1980s, the West End has remained physically intact since the destruction of the St James 50 years ago. Yet theatres aren't primarily pieces of architecture. They are places where shows are delivered to the public; and if some are artistically obsolete, what's their point?

I feel as sentimental as anybody when I enter the Haymarket, Drury Lane or that tiny treasure-house, the Criterion. Yet I worry about their future. The younger dramatists, as we'll see, aren't writing for them. The producers struggle to keep all forty West End theatres filled with potentially profitable work. Many of the more exciting directors shun them. Most are well suited to revivals of

Pinero, Wilde and the Restoration classics; some are right for Andrew Lloyd Webber's *Phantom of the Opera* and other lavish musicals. But can and should the West End subsist on that?

Moreover, the *Zeitgeist* is against them. These theatres' inner architecture exudes the feel of a more graceful, class-bound world than we're likely to inhabit in the years ahead. Already there's something incongruous about finding *Trainspotting* in the Ambassadors, as recently happened, rather than the tiny, informal Bush, where Irvine Welsh's drug-culture novel received its first, most vivid London staging. But what's to be done with the Aldwych, the Gielgud and the other theatres that give my nostalgic side a lift whenever I enter them?

Those that don't go permanently dark, as has happened with some Broadway theatres, will presumably continue to present artistic compromises: more or less acceptable mismatches between playhouse and play. But those who recall Peter Brook's famous categories of theatre – 'deadly', 'holy', 'rough', 'immediate' – will be aware that they are best suited to the first of the four. The 'holy', meaning drama with vision and soul to share, may sometimes thrive in a traditional theatre. But more earthy, direct or disputatious work needs a different environment. A theatre in flight from the lonely pleasures of high-tech living rooms and desperate for life and contact – the theatre of the future – will need places where we can see the actors' eyeballs, hear their breathing, and know they are real.

Chapter 4
A Place for Performance Art?

To say that theatre isn't synonymous with drama hasn't always been a truism. In the 1960s exasperation with traditional forms combined with a more general turbulence to convince some practitioners and critics that 'plays' were old hat. America's Living Theatre made a global reputation by delivering insults ('you bourgeois motherfuckers'), shrill complaints ('I cannot travel without a passport') and hieratic blessings as they touched their audiences ('holy head, holy nose, holy moustache'). And what writer could express the drift towards social chaos as succinctly as the section of Jean-Claude van Itallie's *America Hurrah!* in which huge, smirking dolls wrecked a motel room?

These attempts to push the theatre into an imaginative world where words lost their dramatically familiar functions – sometimes lively, sometimes silly – were generically described as 'performance art' or 'theatre of mixed means'. They incorporated mime, dance, acrobatics, circus skills, puppetry, surreal or Dadaist events, and strange musical, lighting and design effects. Any account of this area which aspired to be complete would acknowledge many figures, among them Grotowski, Tadeusz Kantor, Steven Berkoff, the People Show, Richard Schechner, Andre Serban, and Robert Wilson who, when I met him, eagerly described the *mis-en-scène* of a British piece he'd recently seen, adding 'and then the stupid play started'.

I later realised he was talking about Harold Pinter's *Homecoming*, which has proved more durable than Wilson's *Overture to Ka Mountain*, which lasted longer than the time it took God to create the world, seven days and nights. That is, of course, an unfair comparison, for performance art is transitory, impermanent, hard to notate;

yet it's clear that it has had less widespread impact than some of us expected in the 1960s and has penetrated little into mainstream theatre: meaning Broadway, off-Broadway and their British counterparts.

That's hardly surprising, for most theatre people dedicated to the avant-garde and experimental would find an absurd contradiction in wanting to do anything but avoid the mainstream. Again, there are notable exceptions to the rule. Robert Lepage has brought his *Tectonic Plates* and *Needles and Opium*, as well as his more verbal *Seven Streams of the River Ota*, to the National. Berkoff's imaginatively freewheeling versions of *Salome* and Kafka's *Trial* have appeared there too. But the ending of the Royal Court's annual season of avant-garde theatre, Barclays New Stages, along with the abolition of the Arts Council's Performing Arts Committee, seems significant. Where's the buzz, the juice, in performance art these days? I expect to continue seeing small touring companies presenting strange and sometimes wonderful theatrical constructions and deconstructions. But a truly exciting revival of the theatre of mixed means is hard to foresee.

Partly that's because success in the genre is normally dependent on the drive and imaginative restlessness of individuals such as Berkoff and the Living Theatre's Julian Beck and Judith Malina. Such originals are by definition difficult to breed or imitate. It's also because the social conditions must be congenial. A flowering of performance art as unsettling as that of the late 1960s may have to await comparable unrest, outrage, disorientation and upheaval.

Or is it possible to predict that New Age consciousness, paganism, or whatever, will be impelled to create its own quasi-religious rituals and that these may take a theatrical form? Already there are companies such as Footsbarn who live as tribes or sects, expressing their distaste for this world and their wish for a fresher, purer one through celebratory performance art, like their version of *The Odyssey*. One can imagine ecological activists, 'green' cultists, or people with equally passionate agendas, turning to theatre as a form of protest, self-assertion or even worship. I can't say I relish the prospect of druidical eurythmics and vegetarian liturgies; but my business is prophecy, not prejudgement.

Chapter 5
The Drama and its Future

Dramatic texts may emerge in unconventional ways: from improvisation, as with Mike Leigh's plays, or from field-trips and discussion, as with *Fen*, the East Anglian piece Caryl Churchill wrote with and for the Joint Stock Company. But these works still consist of speech and dialogue. After all, there's no more effective way of embodying ideas and airing issues than through written drama. Moreover, the theatre dramatist can expect far more room for the play of his language, and far more attention from the audience for his words, than his film or television counterparts. You can't imagine Shaw or Stoppard using the screen as his primary medium.

The more we're bombarded by the electronic media, the more we'll crave a theatre where words matter. We'll crave their precision, their subtlety, their power to explore in depth and debate in detail. We'll crave the punch and poetry of the English language. Indeed, playwrights will have a vital task in a world where articulacy, argument and complexity of thought will probably continue to decline. Given the unique power of the theatre, they can help teach people how to listen, rather than passively hear, and how to express their ideas and feelings, rather than indulge in second-hand California-speak or whatever forms of sub-English emerge in the next century.

But what words? We can't predict anything with confidence except, perhaps, that the small, informal theatres of the future won't be particularly hospitable to epic or sweepingly public drama. Yet the touring troupe Shared Experience have staged effective adaptations of Dickens's *Bleak House* and Tolstoy's *War and Peace* on cramped stages. As Sam Mendes is showing at the Donmar in Covent Garden, a small theatre can retain its intimacy and, if the

.cing area expands to thrust the audience to the sides, still leave a lot of space for the performers and their words.

Let's say, then, that the public drama of the future will tend to buttonhole rather than orate, question rather than legislate, implicitly or explicitly involve the audience rather than ignore it. But that still doesn't take prophecy very far. Indeed, there are those who would say prophecy is impossible, because major playwrights parachute suddenly down from the sky rather than truck onstage in job lots. Who could have predicted *Endgame*, say, or Pinter's *Homecoming*?

Yet even works of surpassing originality don't occur in social vacua. The pessimism of an era that had lost its beliefs while acquiring weapons of mass suicide penetrated Beckett's tale of the old tyrant, isolated in a desolate landscape, who can't renounce power or life. The story of the Londoners who welcome home an estranged son and brother, only to transform his wife into a prostitute, expressed the sixties' scepticism about institutions. Others assailed business, politics, the military; Pinter asked sharp, unsentimental questions about the family.

The playwright David Edgar divides the past decades into rough but distinct categories. The late 1950s and the 1960s, when Osborne and Wesker held sway, may be summed up as 'what about the workers?', for it was a period when classes excluded from power at last gave articulate voice to their anger and desires. 'Reform or revolution?' was an overriding theme of the 1970s, for then David Hare, Howard Brenton, Trevor Griffiths, Howard Barker and Edgar himself moved on to the next question. Could those desires be fulfilled without blood and fire? The result was a Theatre of Cataclysm, a set of plays that variously forecast mobs of scavenging youths, a ruthless secret police and, in Brenton's *Churchill Play*, concentration camps for British dissidents. The last of these was written in 1974 and set in 1984, and should be ruefully remembered by any would-be prophet.

As I said before, the 1980s was a surprisingly barren

decade for new drama; but Edgar's one-word summary, 'women', points to its most positive aspect. For reasons still debated – their inability to penetrate a clubbish male institution, or to see themselves as the active verbs dramatic conflict requires, or to think and feel in the ways that the old, rigidly structured plays invited – the majority sex had historically made a far smaller contribution to the theatre than to the novel. But with the growth of Churchill into a major dramatist, and the emergence of Timberlake Wertenbaker, Sharman Macdonald, Charlotte Keatley and others, the balance began decisively to change. To say now that women will write many of our more significant plays in the years ahead, and therefore that the experiences described and attitudes expressed in the theatre will broaden, seems less a prophecy than a truism.

At the start of the 1990s, everyone was asking the same questions. Of those who had created and sustained the dramatic renaissance that began in the mid-1950s, Osborne was soon to die, Arden had fallen silent and Griffiths and Brenton nearly so, Pinter was writing occasional short, bruising plays on political themes, Wesker, Storey and Nichols saw their new work ignored, Stoppard was producing roughly one play every five years. Only Ayckbourn, Hare, Churchill and Edgar were keeping up their usual flow. So who was going to reanimate and refresh the British drama?

At first the answer seemed to be: writers from other English-speaking countries. Ireland produced several promising new dramatists, notably Billy Roche, author of *Belfry*, *Poor Beast in the Rain* and other plays that brought a Chekhovian blend of sympathy and wry humour to a theme that will prove increasingly urgent in the new millennium: the drawn-out death of communities and the values they have embodied. In a world where roots count for less and less, few writers have so rich a resource as Wexford, the town where Roche was born and still lives; so it seems probable that his social relevance will continue to match the quality of his human observation.

Meanwhile, Canada has sent us some striking plays about urban rootlessness. Brad Fraser's *Unidentified Human Remains and the True Nature of Love*, Judith Thompson's *Lion in the Streets* and other such quirkily episodic pieces created an impression of a world gone violently askew, a spiritual madhouse whose inmates were linked by loveless sex, offhand despair, serial killers and telephone answering machines. The millennium was about to end in chaos, to be replaced by God knows what.

That end-is-nigh feel infected some plays by American dramatists, too. *Weldon Rising* by the London-based Phyllis Nagy was a portrait of the New York jungle in which 200-degree temperatures left cars, bridges and the characters fried. The same author's *Strip* ended with earthquakes, infantile screams and the malevolent laughter of a Mephistophelean tycoon. Then there was Tony Kushner's two-part *Angels in America*, a 'gay fantasia on national themes' that involved Aids, corruption, greed and much else. With hallucinations, ghosts and an Angel of Death arriving amid Spielbergian crashes and flashes, it justified its subtitle, *Millennium Approaches*.

The première of Kushner's tragi-comedy in 1991 seemed important for several reasons. With notable exceptions, mainly David Mamet and the ageing Arthur Miller, American playwrights had long shunned public themes. Had the Aids plague lured a new, more politically aware generation of writers from the living room, bedroom and back porch? Was there a place for rich imaginative effects as well as the dogged naturalism that, Sam Shepard excepted, had dominated Off-Broadway as well as Broadway? Was America preparing to greet the twenty-first century with an apocalyptic drama?

It seems not. A few American pieces have had social bite: Howard Korder's *Search and Destroy* and *The Lights*, Han Ong's *L. A. Plays*, and, from Mamet himself, a piece that suggested that, even in a nation where the theatre has become culturally peripheral, drama could sometimes upset and enrage. Performances of *Oleanna*, about a student who destroys a university professor with accusations of sexual harassment, were marked by heckling, walkouts and noisy confrontations outside the theatre. But as we'll see, the obstacles facing any sort of serious theatre in the US remain daunting, and 'the new surrealism' and 'the theatre of apocalypse' have not materialized.

Nor are there signs of them materializing over here. Why, then, do I feel more optimistic about the future of British drama than I have since the early 1970s?

Starting in 1994, continuing through 1995 and 1996, a remarkable number of striking young playwrights emerged in England, mainly from the Royal Court's tiny Theatre Upstairs and a pub-playhouse in West London, the Bush. Their ages ranged from twenty-two to thirty-four, and they had much in common. Their characters drifted around weird cityscapes, where violence was a frequent threat and escape from feelings of entrapment mostly an illusion. But unlike their predecessors, these dramatists had no obvious ideology, no political credo, no social agenda. If their characters launched into generalization, it was more likely to be about drugs or drink than the sins of the Establishment. They observed the urban British quizzically, reported the contradictions they saw, and left the audience to reach its own conclusions.

There are, of course, differences between Samuel Adamson, Jez Butterworth, Joe Penhall, Judy Upton, Nick Grosso, Simon Bent, David Eldridge, Mark Ravenhill, Simon Block, Michael Wynne and Sarah Kane. A complete list of young, fresh arrivals should also include the thirty-one-year-old Jonathan Harvey and the twenty-seven-year-old Martin McDonagh. But Harvey's comedies, notably *Beautiful Thing*, are better categorized among a series of plays that appeared in the mid-1990s, airing questions about the complexities of gender, pondering the 'crisis of masculinity' and provoking the ineffable headline in one paper, 'Stop This Pink Plague of Gay Plays'.

As for the hugely promising McDonagh, his *Beauty Queen of Leenane* and *Cripple of Inishmaan* are set in a rural Ireland where callousness is so institutionalised as not to be recognized by the characters. A possessive mother ruins her daughter's hopes of love, and is destroyed in reprisal; a crippled, desperate boy tries to escape the boredom of the Aran Isles, circa 1934. McDonagh is a Londoner of Irish extraction; but he, too, deals with the twin themes of entrapment and frustration in a fatalistic way. He, too, disconcertingly mixes the dark and the funny. And though his scenes are less terse, his language more lyrical, his story-telling skills greater, he too opts for an episodic style and swift changes of location in *The Cripple*.

But it's what one might dub the Theatre of Urban Ennui that most obviously expresses the feelings of a generation shaped by the 1980s. If one were to derive a capsule play from already performed work, it might involve gangs of girls adrift in a London where criminals dump bits of their rivals in plastic bags, rent boys are casually raped, there's a lively backstreet trade in stolen burglar alarms, and voracious spivs gather beside ageing charabanc drivers dying of a surfeit of porn. These dramatists are stronger on character and situation than conflict, tension and structure, preferring to offer vivid snapshots rather than concoct plots, maybe because plot implies some coherence in people's lives. They relish the oddball, the misfit, the bizarre; but they are troubled by the helplessness and unhappiness they see all around. They are vastly entertaining yet they radiate moral concern. They are Mrs Thatcher's disoriented children.

These dramatists are English; but Scotland has simultaneously produced several plays by slightly older writers – Chris Hannan's *Shining Souls* and *Evil Doers* and Simon Donald's *Life of Stuff* – that are even more scathing about the banality, violence and moral chaos of cities. Several critics described these pieces' blend of hilarity and (occasionally) savagery as Jacobean, though for a minority *The Life of Stuff*, whose whimsies included a hungry pot-head mistaking a severed, withered toe for a sausage, was in questionable taste. There has been a revival of black and sometimes sick comedy in the 1990s – David Beaird's *900 Oneanta* and Tracy Letts's *Killer Joe*, two successful imports from America, are other examples – that has yet to be adequately explained.

Certainly, we can say that dramatists under forty are approaching the new millennium in an uneasy, uncertain yet unsolemn frame of mind. There's a bravado in their evocation of a Britain they regard as being in disarray. Some seek to 'move wild laughter in the throat of death', treating disaster with a breezy glee that may seem nihilistic, callous or morbid, but is perhaps more positive: a rejection of the 'victim' psychology and reaching-for-sympathy that has marked much British drama in the later twentieth century; a truculent assertion of the human determination to survive in the urban jungle.

Why this new movement and will it continue? It couldn't have emerged either without a shared apprehension, puzzlement and dismay among the younger generation or without practical aid. The Royal Court has a Young Writer's Group which encourages playwriting and gives 'workshops' to plays, and in late 1997 had no fewer than sixty aspiring dramatists under commission, among them many from unprivileged backgrounds. As the success of McDonagh in particular shows, the Court is beginning to release what David Hare has called 'the massive untapped creative potential among people who would never normally think of going to the theatre, let alone writing a play'.

The National has a studio that offers new-play readings, workshops and help in finding a public stage. The method has its critics, who think that workshops mean too much input by directors, actors and fellow-writers, and fear that the result must be essentially collaborative plays blandly reflecting the LCD of a theatre's personnel. But McDonagh's *Cripple of Inishmaan*, which progressed from the National's studio to the Cottesloe, hardly lacks a distinctive voice.

Workshops are likely to be the way of the future for

many dramatists, and the future itself seems sure to produce and develop more and more dramatists. Stoppard has said he began writing plays because of the buzz created by John Osborne's *Look Back in Anger* in 1956. Suddenly that dull cultural ghetto, the theatre, had become 'the place to be at'. That excitement, missing for two decades, is back in Britain again – and who can say what the result may be? I would certainly be surprised if McDonagh, Butterworth and Penhall, in particular, didn't evolve into significant talents.

What could obstruct them and those they may inspire? Several things, including BBC radio's decreasing enthusiasm for nurturing new dramatists and noticably greater caution among the financially troubled theatres in the regions and on the London fringe. There is also the example of Anthony Minghella, Hanif Kureishi and other once-promising British playwrights. More may be sucked into television, film or the black hole of Hollywood, which has turned so many American writers into anti-matter. In 1997 Butterworth was actually making a film of his brilliant *Mojo*, and McDonagh was writing a script for Hollywood.

But both still expect to divide their future between film or television and the stage. In Britain, where the theatre's centre isn't 3,000 miles from the movie one, this is easier to manage than in America, as the careers of Stoppard, Hare and Stephen Poliakoff have shown. And if theatre producers sometimes shackle dramatists' imagination by demanding plays with small, inexpensive casts, they can also offer them what Michael Attenborough, who commissions new work for the RSC, calls 'the opportunity to escape the naturalistic straitjacket': far more artistic licence and much more control over their work than screenwriters expect.

There are other reasons for optimism about the future of Britain's young, gifted playwrights. With the National Lottery now free to give 'project' grants to dramatists, more may receive larger fees than the £6,000 that's currently the minimum for a new play at major subsidized houses. And is it true that working for film or television lastingly damages a talent? To give the electronic media their due, some dramatists return to the theatre more aware of the value of silence, understatement and succinct dialogue.

Moreover, dramatists can have a public impact denied to screenwriters. Quite aside from their greater power over a particular audience, they may create a stir disproportionate to the numbers they immediately reach. Ariel Dorfmann's torture-play *Death and the Maiden*, launched at the sixty-seat Theatre Upstairs, reverberated round the world. The theatre makes names, brings the chance of publication and revivals, subjects a writer to critical and even academic scrutiny. A playwright gets the attention the screen offers to directors but very seldom to writers; and often more of it.

That said, what sort of drama can we foresee? In the short term, sharp, scathing, impressionistic plays given extra intensity by being staged in theatres that draw spectators into vivid, mainly urban worlds. But let's not forget the more established dramatists. After a thin 1980s, Pinter has rediscovered his imaginative complexity with *Moonlight* and the shamefully underestimated *Ashes to Ashes*. As *Arcadia* showed, Stoppard's wit has deepened. Ayckbourn has brought his dark humour to over fifty plays, and is still only fifty-eight. There are discerning people who invest hope in writers I may have underrated, notably Terry Johnson and Doug Lucie.

A particularly impressive figure is David Hare, whose more private work, notably *Skylight* and *Amy's View* has grown in depth and whose public voice has increased in authority. The plays that comprised his 'Hare Trilogy', and respectively concerned the Church, the law-and-order system and the Labour Party, proved that the theatre was still central to British culture, such was the outpouring of newspaper comment that greeted their presentation in 1993. The last of these, *Absence of War*, now seems prophetic in its wry suggestion that Labour could win power only by 'becoming Tories'.

The trilogy had a sweep, scope and civic significance that justified its production not merely at a playhouse called the National but in the amphitheatre of the Olivier. For once, the audience was in a position literally similar to that of the ancient Athenians, collectively assembled above actors dealing with matters of concern to the health of the polis. As it happens, Hare is the only major dramatist who continues to proselytize for large theatres and to criticize younger playwrights for avoiding the challenge of large stages. What he doesn't acknowledge, though, is that nobody else is writing big state-of-the-nation plays, and nobody looks like doing so.

But that is, again, a short-term diagnosis. Are there less immediate points to be made about British drama? Well, on the formal front the possibilities are limitless. Every rule and prohibition has joined the neo-classical 'unities' in the ashcan. Plays can consist of consecutive monologues, like Brian Friel's *Faith Healer*, or of a row of figures addressing the audience from a table, as in Wallace Shawn's *Designated Mourner*, or of mixed mime and realism, like Churchill's *The Skriker*.

Again, if one worrying side-effect of a burgeoning video culture may be that theatre audiences will demand more frequent stimulation (Peter Brook says that the average time you can rely on a spectator's attention in Los Angeles is two-and-a-half minutes compared with nine hours in Tokyo), a more positive one is that they will accept speedy jumps of time and place with less strain. In the future a play could consist of nothing but a pair of lips gabbling an autobiography that whizzes unpredictably between past and present. In fact, that play was written some years ago. It is Beckett's *Not I*.

Not I remains, however, unusual in another sense. With Beckett's own *Waiting for Godot* and *Endgame* and Stoppard's *Jumpers*, it's one of a handful of modern plays concerned with metaphysical matters. With religious revivalism rampant in so many nations, could British dramatists start asking questions about the meaning of life *sub specie aeternitatis*? History suggests not. Our dramatists have shunned what E. M. Forster called 'prophetic' as opposed to 'preaching' writing since the mid-seventeenth century. They don't have an ear for metaphysics; they don't live in an era where people feel 'tragically'; and they're writing in a medium best suited to the conflict of individual with individual and the individual with his society.

Yet who can say what the most easily discernible developments will bring from our dramatists? George Steiner, claiming that 'it's noon-time not in the arts but in the sciences', has advocated arts festivals that explain and celebrate 'the dance of the spirit in the sciences'. But however great the exhilaration in the laboratories, it's what emerges from them that will engage non-scientists. Already we are contemplating a world in which our sicknesses, our predilections, even the time of our deaths can be programmed before birth. The rich and not-so-rich may live much longer, while the rest of the world's population multiplies. Science will throw up endless dilemmas, moral and practical – and where will this place that concerned citizen, the dramatist?

Not, I suspect, celebrating the triumph of science but reacting to and possibly against its impact. Dramatists do, after all, tend to be questioners, dissenters, and there will be plenty to question in the twenty-first century. One can foresee plays that emphasize the human animal and sometimes the resilient human spirit beneath the social and scientific construct. One can imagine plays that appeal, more than any being written now, to a deep craving for story-telling, myth and the sense of identity that, in whirligig times, legend and history offer. Less happily, one can foresee plays that reach nostalgically into the 1950s, 1970s or even 1990s, when ethics were supposedly simpler and life more rewarding.

Again, will the world continue simultaneously to shrink and fracture? The global village is with us, yet, thanks to the threat this poses to cultural identity, the village is packed with divided houses and fighting relatives. Homogeneity coexists with aggressive nationalism, creating conflicts that, at least in the theatre, only Edgar's Balkan play, *Pentecost*, has effectively confronted. Will the playwright's function be to debate such conflicts, take sides, remind us of our common humanity, and/or resist encroaching materialism by insisting on the claims of the spirit?

But the future alters even faster than the present, for every change now creates a new set of possible permutations for the years ahead. Imagine an updated version of Aristophanes' *Frogs*. Which dramatist will Dionysus bring back to Britain, assuming it exists, in the mid-twenty-first century? Simon Donald, to reflect the period's confusions, or someone more capable than our current crop of young dramatists of discerning meaning in them? The metaphysician Beckett, the zoologist Pinter, the bravura intellectual Stoppard, the funny-glum Ayckbourn or Simon Gray, or the incisive pundit Hare? Or somebody more unexpected and unsung? After all, who could have prophesied that as resonant a drama as any in the 1990s would be a didactic little thriller first performed in 1945?

Chapter 6
Directors, Classics and Revivals

That thriller was Priestley's *An Inspector Calls*, in which every member of a wealthy family is morally complicit in a young woman's suicide. But Stephen Daldry, who directed, transposed the piece from its original drawing room to a set in which pockets of privilege sprouted from a broken wilderness, added expressionistic effects, and ended up with a ringing indictment of the sins of the century. In 1992, it seemed the most contemporary play in London. The freshest, most significant work, it indicated, might have been written 50, 200, 400 years before.

Hamlet is always contemporary, but *King Lear* has seemed particularly to evoke our Godforsaken era. *Troilus and Cressida*, with its demystification of love and heroism, has encapsulated twentieth century cynicism, and, as staged by Trevor Nunn, the still more neglected *Timon of Athens* has proved remarkably sharp about the greedy, uncaring 1980s. Which Shakespeare play will the future find especially eloquent? Its popularity with directors in the late 1990s leads me to nominate *A Midsummer Night's Dream*, with its emphasis on the unpredictable forces beyond science and below reason.

The late 1980s and early 1990s were a great period for the directing art. It hadn't been so many years since an American critic had complained that all English directors were male, middle-aged and called Peter. And in the early 1980s Peter Hall and Peter Wood were hitting fifty, Peter Brook had left for Paris, and even Trevor Nunn, Terry Hands and Richard Eyre were moving irretrievably into their forties. Where was the new generation? Then, quite suddenly, there was young, fresh, male and female talent for a new millennium: Nicholas Hytner, Declan Donnellan, Daldry, Sam Mendes, Deborah Warner, Katie Mitchell, Matthew Warchus and others.

What do they have in common? One or other of them contradicts every generalization; but virtually all have concentrated on staging revivals, and mainly in modest, intimate surroundings. That has provoked criticism, notably from David Hare, who accused several of them of feeling little responsibility for contemporary writing and fearing 'partners of at least equal intellect and ability who are inconveniently alive and present in the rehearsal room to engage them in fruitful dialogue about the direction of their own ideas'. But his attack wasn't quite fair. If contemporary playwrights aren't producing exciting work, as they mostly weren't between 1980 and 1994, why not look for classic alternatives? The past can be more eloquent about the present than the present itself.

Certainly, Donnellan's revival of Lope de Vega's *Fuente Ovejuna*, like Warner's *Titus Andronicus* and *Electra*, had exceptional power. Mitchell, who specializes in simple, spare productions that generate unexpected intensity, has succeeded in reclaiming Euripides's *Phoenician Women*, Heywood's *A Woman Killed with Kindness* and Githa Sowerby's *Rutherford and Son* from (respectively) millennia, centuries and decades of neglect. Some revivals have been of merely academic interest; but others have brought vibrant work, foreign as well as British, back from the tomb. Who had heard of Marieluise Fleisser until her *Pioneers in Ingolstadt* appeared at the Gate? Who knew much about the Spanish Golden Age until the seasons of representative work at the same theatre?

The search for that paradox, the new classic, will continue; and rightly so. Indeed, I foresee a craving for certain classic plays in the future, for some 'old' dramatists are peculiarly able to fulfil needs our descendants are likely to feel. One is for the strong, bold stories and gripping narrative you don't find in any Theatre of Urban Ennui. Another is for ideas and emotions that a rationalist era regards as naive or primitive.

The Elizabethans and Jacobeans in particular ask you to suspend disbelief in the existence of titanic feelings and absolute values. They ask you to look at fierce, elemental encounters in a universe where the deity, though sometimes worryingly absent, has significance for the characters. And isn't there something invigorating about plays that avoid psychological or social explanations for human conduct and refuse to reduce good and evil into mere virtue and vice? As the behavioural, biological and sociological sciences annex yet more of the spirit, something in us yearns to counter-attack. And what better way will the future find of vicariously fighting reductionism, and asserting the power of emotion and the resilience of mystery, than by reviving the Greek, British and Spanish tragedies with all their blood, magic and exhilarating stoutheartedness?

Even those directors who resist this line of argument will surely agree with another. The inadequacies of our educational system and the globalization of culture are shrinking our vocabulary to the dourly functional and making classic work seem grotesquely garrulous. Peter Hall has said that Shakespeare will soon become incomprehensible enough to need translation; yet anyone who looks at the first authoritative moves in this direction, A. L. Rowse's modernization of Shakespeare's plays, will be struck by the impoverishment that relatively minor changes bring. A major task of future directors will be not to preserve English in aspic, but robustly to demonstrate the vitality, abundance, expressiveness and beauty of the language we have inherited. It will be to join the playwrights of tomorrow in teaching the British to listen, speak, feel and think less thinly.

But it could be replied that richness is the last thing on some directors' minds. At worst, they remake Shakespeare in their own shrivelled images. And that brings me to questions that will continue to preoccupy critics and practitioners. How will the future define the director's function? How far should his or her remit stretch?

Already I sense a reaction against a tyranny that has, after all, existed for barely a century. It's not only Hare who assails 'the wilder excesses of Director's Theatre with all its naff ideas and its opportunities for largely arbitrary pieces of self-advertisement'. The perpetrators as well as the victims are sounding uneasy. Jonathan Miller, who has often tilted classic plays in perverse directions, confesses to despairing of the right strategy for the twenty-first century. He still feels there's no 'canonical version' of a text, no way of fully discovering and fulfilling a play-wright's intentions; yet he's appalled by 'deconstruction-ists' who use texts 'as pretexts for high jinks'.

Similarly, the great Italian director Giorgio Strehler feels that audiences are apt to treat directors as the key creative artists and directors to see themselves as stars: 'You shouldn't go to see what a director thinks about *Hamlet*. You should go in the hope of being given only *Hamlet*, produced and acted artistically.'

Myself, I got a strong inkling of what both men meant when I saw Miller's own 1996 revival of *A Midsummer Night's Dream*, which added Noël Coward fairies to P. G. Wodehouse Athenians in a doggedly rationalist attempt to turn an enchanting play into a droll comment on the British class system. But Miller himself was probably think-ing of the American director Peter Sellars, who declares it 'crazy' to try to discern a writer's intentions. His reason for staging *The Merchant of Venice* was rather to express 'what it feels like at this moment to be here in this world and the pain of a sense of a system that's out of control'. The production itself, which visited London in 1994, turned out to be Sellars's own gloss on the Los Angeles race riots, on gender wars, and, with Bassanio humping Antonio on the floor of the Doge's court, on the problems of bisexuality.

Let's concede that comparably strained revivals are rare, and that even they sometimes come from defensible motives. There's scant excuse for highly tendentious pro-ductions of Shakespeare in America, where he is so seldom seen; but in Britain he's staged often enough for directors to feel a pressure to bring some originality to their work. After all, more orthodox revivals will soon redress any artistic imbalance. Again, what's wrong in trying to make the classics relevant? Is a pedantic academicism better?

There are directors capable of answering these questions wisely and, since they include some of the most gifted, I'm relatively optimistic about classic production in the earlier twenty-first century. If it's impossible fully to discern a dramatist's intentions, it's usually possible (Hare's helpful formulation) to see a play as 'something which works in an intended area of meaning'. And Brook, Peter Stein, Hall, Nunn, Donnellan, Mitchell and others do see their task as investigative rather than prescriptive or editorializing. They are (Stein) 'elder brothers' or (Donnellan) 'coaches', helping actors explore character and situation as deeply as possible, discussing with them what works and what doesn't, and allowing 'concepts' to emerge organically.

But is this to ask the directors of the future to 'play safe'? That phrase can be an underhand way of justifying the flashy and fashionable. Which is 'safer', the unconventional *Coriolanus* that reduces the protagonist to a goose-stepping Hitler, easy to hate, or the one that acknowledges the difficulty of summing up as a 'fascist' the dangerously contradictory figure Shakespeare created? Yet it would be mad to deny that adventurous, unorthodox productions sometimes venture nearer the heart of a play than one striving conscientiously to descry an author's intentions. The *Midsummer Night's Dream* Robert Lepage staged at the National in 1992 was unevenly acted, poorly spoken, not very funny, and wonderful, for, by setting the play in a weird, watery subworld, the Canadian director brought out the dark, unsettling magic beneath the comic surface.

I myself once took a conservative view of productions that wrenched classic plays out of their original periods. I have since recanted, partly because it's foolish to defend a line that's now breached more often than not, but mainly because it was a superficial way of addressing the true problem. That's whether a director diminishes a play by too heavily slanting or conceptualising it. The objection to Jonathan Miller's *Tempest* was not what it was but what it wasn't. By setting the action in Captain Cook's time, turning Ariel into Jomo Kenyatta with a flywhisk, and everywhere stressing colonial parallels, Miller missed the richness of the original. By concentrating on the plays' 'topical' aspects, some modern-dress revivals of Shakespeare leave swathes of character, idea and feeling unexplored.

Despite the excrescences that will doubtless pop through the cracks, this view is widely enough held to constitute a pattern for the future. It is not, let me repeat, a recipe for creative cowardice nor a prescription for slavishly conventional treatment of foreign classic work. Annie Castledine's 1995 production of Euripides' *Women of Troy* with its intimations of Vietnam and Bosnia, wasn't a total success, largely because it was staged in the huge Olivier Theatre; but the play was palpably worth reviving, the approach seemed justified, and Kenneth McLeish's text brought the characters' sufferings vividly to life. Laurence Boswell's revival of the same dramatist's *Electra, Orestes* and *Iphigenia in Tauris* proved more immediate and riveting, because another brilliant translation by McLeish coincided with simple staging in the tiny Gate.

Translation is, incidentally, a bullish art these days. Without changing sense or tone, writers have won an important freedom. That's to shun period pastiche and opt for a direct, accessible English. After all, why should ancient Greeks or the seventeenth-century French speak like stilted Victorians rather than modern men or women? The results have sometimes been alarmingly colloquial, as when Orestes yells 'bastard' at Menelaus or Cassandra laments that 'for one fuck they squandered a million lives'; but such lines can invigorate the drama without distorting the dramatist. All translation involves compromise with the original and loss; but McLeish, Ranjit Bolt and Jeremy Sams, as well as the veteran Michael Meyer and Michael Frayn, have done as much as any director to ensure what matters: that the Greeks, Molière, Ibsen and Chekhov will retain their freshness, punch and wit in the future.

Chapter 7
Technology, Design and Musicals

In mid-1997 Britain's most highly regarded touring theatre, Cheek by Jowl, announced that it would soon suspend its operations for what its founders, Declan Donnellan and Nick Ormerod, called 'a period of reflection resulting in a new company for the millennium'. It would be surprising, however, if radical change ensued, for Cheek by Jowl is already a fine model for the future. Its productions of the classics, for instance a *Duchess of Malfi* set in the 1920s, have reconciled authenticity and power with modernity. It has also evolved remarkably thorough, unBritish creative methods. In Paris, Ariane Mnouchkine expects rehearsals to last four and a half months. At the Schaubühne in Berlin, Peter Stein regarded six months as the norm, and, when he became theatre director of the Salzburg Festival in 1991, was shocked to get only six or seven weeks. But even that would seem a luxury to most British directors, who can seldom rely on much more than a month.

But Cheek by Jowl opts for continuous preparation. After the performers have completed six weeks in the rehearsal room, they regularly convene to test new ideas, explore situations further and change the production as it moves from city to city. They have even scheduled rehearsals on the last day of a seven-month world tour. As a result, they have become virtually the only British group that can claim to be not merely a company but an ensemble. True, the cast may change from production to production; but Donnellan's direction and Ormerod's design are permanent features, and the same actors frequently perform for them. Moreover, their methods bond them so effectively that, if 'ensemble' means a troupe with the time and mutual understanding to transform disparate people into an organic whole, Cheek by Jowl is a serial ensemble.

Is this a pattern others will copy? Well, not every group has the desire or finance for the tours that permit such an ensemble to emerge. Cheek by Jowl's *Duchess of Malfi* couldn't easily be replicated even by the national companies, given the turnover of productions and the demands on performers of a repertoire system. Yet there's one area in which, though it's far from unique, Cheek by Jowl sets standards. That's its simplicity of presentation.

The set for *The Duchess* consisted of little but black drapes and a patterned floor. Not all Ormerod's designs for his company are that spare, but, as he has said, great classic writers so effectively paint their own scenes through words that 'nothing more is needed than the actor and, say, something to sit on'. And here, too, Cheek by Jowl's methods are artistically helpful. With most building-based companies key decisions about the set often have to be made before rehearsals start. Ormerod is always intimately involved with a production, and can decide very late what decor a play requires and alter it even after opening night. For him, it's 'a case of paring down to the essentials, cutting back until you discover what you need'.

Yet a visitor to London who went to Wyndham's for Cheek by Jowl's *Duchess*, and then saw *Miss Saigon* or *Starlight Express*, would have concluded that we live in contradictory times. Indeed, the extremes move further apart by the day. Technology is making ever more elaborate stage effects ever easier to achieve; yet some of the theatre's most creative people are embracing a theatrical Luddism. What will the future make of the possibilities open to it?

A helicopter rises in *Miss Saigon*. Mountains of debris swing and lock together, like copulating dinosaurs, to form barricades in *Les Misérables*. After experiencing the intricate dazzle of *Starlight Express*, the composer Jule Styne talks of 'whistling the lightbulbs'. And in Dave Clark's sci-fi morality *Time*, green lasar beams spatter the stage; metal pods descend to the glare of a landing spaceship; and out of a giant Fabergé egg emerges Akash the Ultimate Word of

Truth: Laurence Olivier made three-dimensional and articulate by film and audio-tape. 'Through your own thoughts
you can create your own universe,' he intones, his solem-
nity undercut by a nose that has slipped to his upper lip,
giving the moving sculpture a shark-like look.

That show appeared in 1986, cost a then record £4
million, and italicizes some points that will remain relevant in the future. Visual glitter and technological bravura
are usually to be found in large-scale musicals. The genre's
audiences expect lavish spectacle and, given the multi-seat
theatres usually involved, it's the only form capable of
generating the profits that make lavish spectacle afforda-
ble. But high-tech effects can camouflage remarkably banal
content. Indeed, they can become an end in themselves
instead of a means through which wonderful stories are
conveyed.

Yet let nobody sneer at the advances already made.
Someone can sit before a screen, tap a computer key and
conjure up typhoons, moonscapes, flickering skyscrapers
or enormous explosions dead on cue. A cannon ball can be
heard whizzing across the stage so realistically that the
spectators duck. A tiny star can instantaneously become a
vast dawn. In *Beauty and the Beast* an ogre transmutes into
a prince in a twinkling. The effects in the musical *Martin
Guerre*, among them the burning of a village, were achieved
with the help of giant wooden frames capable of receiving
radio signals, rolling anywhere onstage, twisting, and
never being more than half an inch out of true.

Peter Roberts, who developed this, expects dramatic
advances in the use of lasers and holograms too. We may
soon watch that cannon ball whizz across stage in synch
with its sound and to the accompaniment of terrifying
streaks of coloured light. Otherwise he expects mainly to
see the refinement of what's been achieved. Progress, he
emphasizes, comes in response to need. And sensational
effects 'must always be a show's servant, never its master'.

That was true of *Martin Guerre*, whose director and
designer were Donnellan and Ormerod, on furlough from

Cheek by Jowl. But it's more dubiously the case with the Disney Organization's *Beauty and the Beast*, at £10 million the most expensive show yet staged in Britain, and it certainly wasn't so with another American mega-musical, *Big*, which cost and lost $12 million in 1994. Directors and designers can end up paying so much attention to spectacular technology, for instance a $100,000 piano with lights that flashed and notes that sounded as *Big*'s actors danced on its keys, that mere human matters get neglected. Tim Rice believes his musical *Chess* failed precisely because too much was spent on an 'over the top set'.

Yet Rice also says that '99.9 per cent of the people on this ghastly planet want to see huge mega-musicals and couldn't give a stuff even what language they're in'. That remark, like those sets, seems over the top. Some of Andrew Lloyd Webber's and Boublil and Schonberg's grandest creations continue to enjoy huge success in both London and New York. Some people crave the visual astonishment that led nineteenth-century producers to stage shipwrecks or rail crashes. But film will remain better at satisfying this hunger. You can't easily imagine *Independence Day* or *Jurassic Park* onstage. In any case, the days of the big pop opera may be numbered.

Lloyd Webber has himself said that the cost of musicals has reached 'really dangerous levels', that the technology is 'totally out of control', and that after *Les Mis* and *Phantom of the Opera* 'people have started to look for something different in scale'. But as the impresario Cameron Mackintosh emphasizes, this is an area where prediction is always folly. *Oklahoma!*, *No No Nanette* and *Oliver!* were all expected to fail, and *Porgy and Bess* initially did so. Though I suspect that what might be called the international theme-park show will continue to surface – the director David Pountney has half-jokingly forecast a clutch of huge music theatres built beside Heathrow – I expect to see more intimate musicals, maybe even boasting books instead of quasi-operatic padding between the numbers.

That Lloyd Webber's *By Jeeves!* failed when it was pretentiously staged in the huge acreage of Her Majesty's and delighted everyone when it received a modest, rough-theatre production may only prove that there are some subjects better suited to small rather than large playhouses. Yet his *Whistle Down the Wind* would have enjoyed a more successful premiere if it had opened somewhere less ample than Washington's National Theatre in 1996, and his *Joseph and the Amazing Technicolour Dreamcoat*, hideously tarted up for the London Palladium, would surely regain its charm somewhere akin to the school stage for which it was written.

As Sam Mendes has shown with *Assassins* and *Company* at the Donmar, Stephen Sondheim best fits a theatre intimate enough to allow his lyrics to be enjoyed. Should composer-librettists of comparable calibre emerge in the future, the same will prove true for them. Clever, witty words aren't well served by the blare of a sung-through, highly miked score. Nor is nuance of situation and character, feeling or thought. Nor is give-and-take between spectator and performer. Ian Judge, who felt the audience became far more involved when he staged *Showboat* without amplification, believes that the next generation will be writing serious human-scale musicals. Only the continuing need to find product for London and Broadway's bigger theatres leads me to wonder if his conclusion needs qualifying.

But it would be absurd to imply that visual bravura and high-tech wizardry are confined to mega-musicals. Indeed, it's wrong to equate the two. Advanced technology can sometimes permit a greater simplicity of staging plays. Subtly used light – digital beams, computerized coloured gels, *et al.* – can and increasingly will replace décor. Conversely, attention-grabbing sets may exist without electric winches, fibre-optic cables and so on. That was often demonstrated during the design explosion that stretched from the later 1980s into the 1990s.

With such talents as Ormerod, MacNeil, Mark Thompson, Robin Don and Tim Hatley joining John Napier, Bob

Crowley and other established figures, designers at last received widespread recognition. Their influence on the style and nature of a production had always demanded it, and it was increasingly clear that their imaginations deserved it. The designer–director, notably Philip Prowse at the Glasgow Citizens, made an occasional appearance. People began to talk of a Designer's Theatre, much as they had spoken of a Director's Theatre, and with similar qualms.

If designers sometimes overelaborated, it wasn't necessarily to flaunt their skills. There were large theatres that looked cavernous and forlorn without decisive visual effects. Yet I recall a production of Molière's *Bourgeois Gentilhomme* that filled the Olivier with so much surreal grandiosity, including a stretch-limo piano with twenty legs, that the ensuing satire of social climbing seemed almost redundant. I also remember a revival of Shakespeare's *Pericles* that swamped the same stage with effects derived from Inca, Inuit, Sufi, African and Haitian civilizations. One designer read us an editorial on the play; the other opted for visual overkill, destroying the emotional core of a touching play.

Crowley has attacked overblown, heavily 'conceptual' design: 'If the curtain goes up and it's a play about anarchy, and the stage is set at a ridiculous angle, the walls are falling in and there's a pile of masonry on the set, you think so what? We might as well go home. All you've done is give the audience a metaphor for what's about to take place.' He believes décor needn't be numbingly naturalistic. It can be exciting, vivid, even heightened. But it shouldn't overwhelm the performers. There should be space and room for the audience to 'complete the picture' through its imagination: 'there has to be a kind of communion, otherwise you might as well stay home and watch TV'.

That surely indicates the way the best design will go. The intimate stages and closely involved audiences of the future won't need abundant, emphatic décor. They'll require visual hints, imaginative nudges. Already actors often find that they themselves are in effect the set, and that their words and gestures conjure up the world they inhabit. The result is a freedom of movement and a fluency particularly helpful to classic production. The light changes, a new actor enters, and we instantly accept that Forres is Inverness, or Fife has become London. Increasingly the theatre is trusting its audiences to furnish spaces, and, unless we are talking of mega-musicals and sensation-seekers, its audiences seem delighted to do so.

That way, the theatre does something film and television cannot. It reminds us that we possess a visual imagination and stretches it for us. In a high-tech world, where holograms may one day dance from our living-room walls, this will become increasingly valuable. The theatre may be the last place where we can gather together and, helped by a few actors, construct dreams and share fancies. It will be a gymnasium for underused imaginations.

Let me re-emphasize that this isn't to reject either beauty of design or technological innovation. If Sellars' use of cameras and screens to give close-ups of faces in *The Merchant* was awkwardly done, the idea is bound to resurface. Robert Lepage has often exploited video, film and complex stage machinery to creative effect. Yet this same Lepage deplores the over-programming of theatre: 'People want live risks. They need to see people dropping the ball once in a while to be reassured there's human beings playing the game, that what you're going to see is authentic because it's just happening that evening.' Maybe Lepage's most important contribution is to demonstrate that strange, spectacular effects can occasionally be reconciled with human immediacy and complex technology subsumed into rough theatre.

Rough theatre is an inexact term. Maybe it's just a reformulation of the truism that all that's needed for a play is passion and a plank. For me, it means seeing an actor in an oatmeal robe holding a flower on a timber stage, and being convinced that this is God in the Garden of Eden. Katie Mitchell and her designer, Vicki Mortimer, achieved that in their 1997 staging of English mystery plays. It means evoking the farms and hills of France with a sprinkling of pails, chopping blocks, an old table, a tin bath. That was *The Three Lives of Lucie Cabrol* as created by the Théâtre de Complicité, Britain's leading exponents of the art of making much out of little. It's a kind of theatre I expect to see much more often in the future.

Chapter 8
The Actors of the Future

In 1997 we went forward to the past. Shakespeare's Globe, or as precise a replica as scholarship could conceive, opened in London with *Henry V*. Apart from flood lighting when night came, technology was banished. Décor and props were kept at a minimum, which meant that, as in Shakespeare's day, the audience had to imagine that a wooden O was Britain or France. And since the groundlings might move to the edge of the stage, the actors couldn't chat realistically to each other. They had to reach out and up to spectators standing below and seated in narrow tiers above.

Nobody yet knows how much the Globe will add to Britain's cultural life. Nor is a highly distinctive theatre open to the sky likely to be copied elsewhere. Yet the theatre seemed almost futuristic in the demands it made on performers. Actors may not always have to acknowledge the audience as directly as in the Globe, a playhouse where 'To be or not to be' will be less a private monologue, more a shared confidence. But more intimate theatres, more give-and-take with the spectators, barer stages, and more space to exploit will require remarkably complete actors.

Do we have them, will we get them? The evidence of major foreign directors, who can compare nation with nation, is interestingly mixed. Lluis Pasqual feels that British actors are 'fantastic': open, generous and so ready to unloose their inner demons onstage that 'when I see theatre in England, I think "how much money they must save on psychiatry"'. Yet directing *The Dream* at the National left Lepage thinking 'the actors' voices were amazing and they had this way of working with words, but it was from the neck up. When you try to incarnate th in their bodies and make them move, just forget it.' Lev Dodin of St Petersburg's Maly Theatre mourns 'a great reserve of energy' in British players he thinks goes unused, yet Yukio Ninagawa thinks that they 'can be almost animalistic'.

My nose is probably pressed too close to the stage to disentangle all this. But in forty years of theatregoing I've seen, not only an unending parade of often exhilarating talent, but an evolution in acting. British players have become more comfortable with their bodies, physically more expressive, emotionally bolder; and all without compromising such traditional strengths as vocal adroitness, intellectual incisiveness, a sense of irony and serio-comic texture, and the discipline to subject the ego to the good of the whole.

Of course, this is a relative claim. Russians tend to be physically more ebullient, Germans more punctilious, Americans emotionally more self-revealing. But to see John Malkovich in Lanford Wilson's *Burn This*, brilliantly hawking up feeling without regard for the production's balance, was to feel grateful that so many British actors have found a creative haven between Method self-indulgence and frosty articulacy. Peter Hall once said that the English theatre was 'a company of a thousand players' regularly working together; and I could instantly name a hundred who lift my spirits whenever I see them on a cast-list. With Emma Fielding, Victoria Hamilton, Toby Stephens and Rufus Sewell ready to take the baton that has been passing from the Olivier to the Scofield to the McKellen to the Sher generation, the future of acting is in excellent hands.

But some will find this assessment smug, and for several reasons. The increasing inability of regional reps to afford to stage Shakespeare and other classic dramatists means that young performers aren't developing such skills as handling dramatic poetry. And then there's the lure of television, likely to become stronger as stations, series and soaps multiply. Moreover, there are major or potentially major stage players – Anthony Hopkins and Emma Thompson for instance – who have found fame and fortune in the movies. Others will doubtless follow.

This isn't yet as damaging a problem as it is in the US, where geography forces many performers to choose between Hollywood and New York. But from Vanessa Redgrave to Ralph Fiennes, many British actors have managed to achieve success on both screen and stage, often using their earnings from the one to sustain them on the other.

Yet some drama-school teachers worry about the future. One of the most senior says that students regard Pacino and de Niro the way their predecessors did Olivier or Ashcroft, usually get their first jobs on television, and often expect to make their careers in the electronic media. He also has his doubts about the psyche of our future actors.

Like the dramatists currently creating a Theatre of Urban Ennui, they grew up in a period of uncertainty in the workplace, instability in the family, belief in the primacy of the individual, scepticism about social solutions and, maybe, more trust in computer buttons than hard work. The result, I'm told, can be an odd mixture of insecurity and immaturity, egoism and fear. Many drama students seem frightened of committing themselves intellectually or emotionally, and dislike standing out of the group; yet they are impressed by celebrity, crave fame, and seem less eager to work with and for each other than earlier generations. The women tend to have 'little girl voices', and both sexes to regard standard English as 'posh'. Some drama schools are having to reassert a virtue they had thought old-hat: articulacy.

Perhaps the academies will deal with these problems before they become entrenched obstacles to excellence. Certainly, I myself haven't yet noticed obvious weaknesses among our younger actors. Indeed, there's evidence that the increasing attention the academies are giving to voice and movement is producing a generation able to sing and dance as well as act. Moreover, a company like Théâtre de Complicité is encouraging performers to bring a gymnastic resourcefulness to their acting. If the actors of the future will themselves have to substitute for décor on bareish stages, they will increasingly need these strengths. A simpler, rougher theatre will demand performers who can bounce us into believing they are trees, tigers or Tamburlaines – and yet still have the heart and guts to bring Masha or Macbeth fully to life.

A model for the future may be Kathryn Hunter, the tiny actress who has transformed herself into a human praying mantis as the sinister protagonist of Durrenmatt's *Visit* for the Théâtre de Complicité and played King Lear for the West Yorkshire Playhouse. Her blend of intensity and physical inventiveness is still unusual; yet she has had mainstream recognition, including an Olivier award for *The Visit*. Her Lear raises an obvious question, too. Has cross-gender casting a significant future?

Again, it's a question of whether a performer has the commitment and power to shake away our disbelief. Max Beerbohm dismissed Sarah Bernhardt's Hamlet as 'très grande dame'; but then she was an old, lame woman acting for a late-Victorian audience. Frances de la Tour's Prince was more warmly received. In 1996, Fiona Shaw played Richard II at the National, emphasizing the character's immaturity and playfulness rather than some 'feminine' side. Hunter's Lear was old, frail and plausibly male. Each time I found myself arguing with the interpretation, not the hidden gender, and each time I felt sympathy for the endeavour itself. Glenda Jackson left the theatre for politics partly because she didn't want 'to stick around in order to play the Nurse in *Romeo and Juliet*'. Good roles are in short supply for ageing actresses. In a world that claims to be increasingly gender-blind, maybe there's a case for giving our more resourceful women, if not a crack at Coriolanus, the chance to explore the interstices of the subtler roles. Who wouldn't wish to see Eileen Atkins's Iago or Prospero?

Gender-blind casting, however, remains rare. Colourblind casting is another matter. Who could object to this after seeing Josette Simon as Marilyn Monroe in Arthur

Miller's *After the Fall*, or Hugh Quarshie's Tybalt, or A[d]
Lester in Sondheim's *Company*? Sadly, some still do. W[]
Clarence Smith played the King of France in *Lear* at
Stratford, he was barracked by a Frenchwoman as 'an insult
to France'. He wasn't wearing a red nose or making funny
faces, but, like Simon, Quarshie and Lester, he is black. So
is Clive Rowe, whose casting as a New Englander in a
revival of *Carousel* provoked criticism from the literal-
minded.

But there seemed to be nothing but applause for Rowe's
Nicely-Nicely and Clarke Peters' Sky Masterson in the
National's 1996 *Guys and Dolls*. In neo-classical times
audiences found leaps of location or time unacceptable.
That's why Dryden transposed *Antony and Cleopatra* to
Alexandria, reduced its span to a few hours, and called the
result *All for Love*. But we have recovered our ability to
suspend disbelief, and, as I keep emphasizing, the theatre
of the future will ask us to push imaginative consent even
further. If we can accept that a woman with a cart on a
bare stage is Mother Courage plodding through Europe, or
a few crates are a farm, or Kathryn Hunter is Lear, we
shouldn't find it hard to agree that emotional truth is more
than skin deep. As Dr Johnson long ago argued, 'delusion,
if delusion be admitted, has no certain limitation'.

This wisdom is, however, more commonly accepted at
the National, RSC and other subsidized theatres than in
the West End. Blacks and Asians still find it difficult to
develop satisfying acting careers; yet they account for
roughly one-tenth of drama school students and over
1,000 of them belong to the actors' trades union, Equity.
Gifted British actors and actresses with classical training
can hardly be required contentedly to keep playing nurses
and spivs on TV. This is an urgent question for the future,
as, maybe paradoxically, is that of black companies. Talawa
and the Black Theatre Co-op have had their moments, but
only the Asian group, Tara, has maintained a long-term
reputation for consistent excellence. Will the next century
not only see more minority actors penetrating the main-

stream but produce people with the drive to create a permanent theatre for a permanent black company?

Another question. Will we see more mixed-nationality work? Peter Brook has pioneered this at his Paris headquarters. He regularly brings European, Asian and African actors into the same cast in the belief that, with each adding something distinctive from his background, environment and theatrical tradition, a production's 'blood and cream' will be enriched. But Britain has yet to produce anything to compare with a *Mahabharata* and *Cherry Orchard* that could be performed either in English or French. In 1996 Vanessa and Corin Redgrave's Moving Theatre staged an *Antony and Cleopatra* that reminded one London critic of 'a scratch multi-lingual, multi-racial company recruited from the United Nations amateur dramatic society in a bad year'.

But, unlike the Redgraves, Brook has the time and personnel to bind diverse nationalities into an authentic whole. Another difference is that the Redgraves had a socio-political agenda, and Brook has an artistic one. Yet of course those aims aren't irreconcilable. Strehler founded the Théâtre de l'Europe in Paris to help ensure that, as the Continent achieved economic and political union, its complex cultural identity shouldn't be forgotten. The results have included a *Threepenny Opera* with French, German, Polish and Italian actors, and a *Midsummer Night's Dream* in which performers from nine nations spoke their own languages. According to Strehler, there will soon be a generation of bilingual or trilingual actors to 'form the basis for a new European theatre'.

That sounds questionably appealing and, given our mistrust of the EU and linguistic deficiencies, of less relevance to Britain than to mainland Europe. Yet Strehler also emphasized that he didn't foresee a 'standardized' European theatre. Different theatres would draw on their own traditions and play in their own languages. He looked forward to a Europe of 'diversity and particularity', where there would be 'an ever more meaningful exchange of

ideas, talent, ability, methods and styles'. That wou
political as well as artistic impact, for it would be a
source of strength to sustain our common huma
culture which is today suffering a profound crisis'. Actors,
like the Latin-speaking travellers of yore, would bring the
best that is thought and felt to a fragmented Europe.

Paris is the centre of this endeavour, for London has
never been as hospitable, financially or otherwise, to individual genius. There, the internationally minded innova-
tors include not only Brook but Ariane Mnouchkine,
director of the Théâtre du Soleil, in which up to twenty
nationalities are represented. She has declared that 'my
theatrical parents are India, Japan and China' and staged
an adaptation of Aeschylus, *Les Atrides* that thrillingly
combined the French language with an Oriental style.

British actors haven't yet been much involved in pan-
European or international productions – Michael Sheen's
Peer in Ninagawa's Oriental-Occidental *Peer Gynt* is an
exception – but thanks especially to the Edinburgh Festival, the London International Festival of Theatre and the
impresario Thelma Holt, they are sometimes able to see
foreign performers. In the late 1990s I myself have
reviewed work from the Ukraine, Georgia, Romania, Brazil,
Poland, Palestine and South Africa. Whether our actors
have taken these opportunities is another matter. Whatever their own theatregoing, wherever they end up performing, the more complete actors the future will demand
cannot afford to be insular.

Chapter 9
Finance and the Dangers Ahead

Will our creative people get the chance to become complete? Every hope I've expressed may be stymied by the failure of government to give the statutory funding bodies the modest sums necessary to ensure the theatre's future.

The successes of the past forty years surely prove that public funding is essential to the theatre as a whole. Time was, the commercial impresarios regarded the subsidized sector as 'unfair competition'. But who should be contributing to the Arts Council's 1995–6 annual report but the most successful West End producer of all? It's Cameron Mackintosh who now argues that British theatre is 'the envy of the world' only because public money has been invested in companies that have taught everyone from actors to technicians their craft. The West End itself is dependent not only on direct imports from the subsidized sector, such as the National's *Inspector Calls* or the RSC's *Les Misérables*, but on individuals, from Stoppard to Hall, Judi Dench to John Napier, who honed their skills there.

There's a broad consensus in Britain, as there isn't in the US, that a thriving theatre merits state and municipal help. But the Thatcher years brought squeezes and cuts, and demonstrated that the theatre's future is frighteningly dependent on the vicissitudes of politicians. Give our theatre people a sympathetic, moderately generous administration, and the sky's the limit. Elect a penny-pinching government in 2002, or whenever, and the theatre will wither – with knock-on effects for the American theatre, the movie industry and television.

Consider the Parnassus Playhouse in Coketown. Thirty years ago, the theatre boasted a twelve-person ensemble, and presented an impressive diversity of work in its main house, plus striking new plays in its studio. It often mounted productions of special interest to its community, and had a thriving 'outreach' team, which visited local schools and organized theatre for young people.

But the Regional Arts Board that since devolution has substituted for the Arts Council has cut Parnassus' grant, and a financially embattled Coketown City Council has done likewise. Fiscal pressures have led the theatre to divert resources from production budgets to marketing and PR; but the Sponsorship Officer cannot find the philanthropists to cover his own salary. The theatre has a deficit of £1 million, has closed its studio, has raised ticket prices and therefore lost audiences; it no longer has a permanent company, seldom stages plays with casts of more than five, has fired many of its experienced technical staff, and has abandoned its outreach programme; it has cut its productions from ten to four a year, developed an enthusiasm for adaptations of Jane Austen, and expects increasingly to become a 'receiving' house, taking in touring work. Persistent shortage of subsidy has left Parnassus barely worthy of subsidy.

Even if no regional rep is in quite this capsule pickle, there are theatres from Sheffield to Farnham, Salisbury to Bristol, which would recognise that picture. There are problems other than finance, such as the decreasing willingness of actors to work outside London. Yet wouldn't they more often do so if reps could afford more than the Equity minimum of £225 a week?

It isn't as if these theatres have ignored government calls to rid themselves of a 'welfare state mentality'. Business sponsorship has been a modest success for the conspicuous and fashionable, notably the RSC and the National, but accounts for only 4 per cent of the income of the subsidized theatre overall. The latest salve, work mounted in collaboration with other theatres, brings longer rehearsal and playing time; but the evidence is that it doesn't significantly decrease costs and often results in bland productions that don't reflect the artistic identity of any of the playhouses involved.

This matters not only to the communities involved. If the network of reps created over many years deteriorates further, where will the acting, directing and designing talent of the future develop? And the situation seems hardly less precarious in the West End itself. Consider the case of young Wood B. Producer. His pet play has a cast of ten and, with marketing costs alone approaching £100,000, will cost £250,000 to stage; the owners are asking £21,000 a week for the use of a suitable theatre; the TV star he must cast to be sure of a public wants a weekly £7,000 and will commit for three months only; and his potential 'angels' are nervous of a piece that must take £45,000 a week to cover its running costs and sell 70 per cent of seats for nearly four months to make any profit. So Wood opts for a 'compendium' show called *Cliff Edge*, in which one performer bops about delivering the songs of our premier showbiz knight.

Again, that's scarcely an exaggeration. There's a danger of the West End dwindling into the play-free zone Broadway virtually is already. Several small theatres in New York are almost permanently dark, because they haven't the seats both to meet high running costs and recoup production costs that can be over $1 million for a straight play and vastly more for a musical. True, the statistics make superficially good reading. During the season 1996–7, ten million people paid a record $490 million to see Broadway shows. But only thirty-seven productions opened, half as many as two decades before, and almost all were revivals or musicals. Analysis of a characteristic week in 1997 showed that eighteen musicals accounted for eighty-nine per cent of the $8.4 million taken in the twenty-six (out of a total of thirty-eight) Broadway theatres that weren't dark.

Is this the future for the West End, with its forty-odd theatres? Not at once. Work normally costs less than half to produce. Theatres aren't often dark. There were 115 new productions in 1996, though that figure included offerings at the subsidized National, RSC and Royal Court. Over eleven million people paid £229 million at the box-office to see many more performances than were on offer in New York. The top ticket for a big musical was £32.50 compared with $75 or £46 on Broadway, where audiences increasingly consist of the older, wealthier and more conservative.

Yet costs and seat prices in the West End rose greatly in the 1980s and early 1990s, and predictions are that the average age of its audiences will be markedly higher by 2006. And already musicals dominate the scene. Modern drama took £9.4 million at West End box offices in 1996, compared with £138 million for musicals; and that figure would be a lot lower without the returns from the National, RSC and Court. Peter Brook's prophecy that the Broadway season will eventually consist of one multi-million musical, watched by one senile zillionaire paying a billion for his seat, seems less relevant to London; but the danger-signs are there.

But then the main difference between America and Britain is the existence of public subsidy. Its virtually complete absence explains many of the New York theatre's weaknesses, including its lack of anything to compare with Britain's National and RSC. Yet at the time of writing both companies were enduring years of standstill in their grants, meaning real-term cuts and serious financial pressure. The National had just changed its artistic director, though Trevor Nunn was vowing to maintain Richard Eyre's successfully catholic policy. The RSC's outlook seemed more uncertain; and not only because it had accumulated a £1.6 million deficit. Though it was retaining its base in Stratford, it was substituting regional 'residencies' for its six-month summer seasons in London. Will this reduce access to its work and deter top actors from joining the company, thereby lowering its quality? The answer to this is vital, for the RSC, like the National, ought to continue to be one of Britain's glories in the coming century.

Yet it seems absurd to have worries about any subsidized theatre. After all, the National Lottery is in full flow, and had provided the arts with £639 million by November 1996. The beneficiaries ranged from Breakout Theatre, which got £15,430 for a van, to the Royal Court, which received £16 million to renew its deteriorating building. The trouble then was that Lottery money was confined to capital projects, which meant that a financially-pressed Court still could barely afford a new copying machine, let alone lavish money on fresh work. The prospect was of countless new facilities nobody could use: 'stainless steel kitchens for a famine', as Eyre put it. Though the Lottery had raised no less than £286 million for the theatre by late 1997, that was and is still the danger.

True, the rules were slightly relaxed in 1996, notably with a scheme called Arts for Everyone, which allowed Lottery money to go to projects which, among other things, 'encouraged new audiences to experience high-quality arts activity' and 'supported new work and helped to develop its audience'. It was a peculiarly British solution, which didn't directly address the core problems of theatres, yet held out the prospect of them finding the money for the odd exciting play, somewhat relieving their budgets and stemming their artistic decline.

So was it a solution at all? Will and should the government go further, and, when we possess new and renovated theatres in abundance, hand all theatrical funding to the Lottery? That is unlikely to happen immediately, for the administration elected in 1997 is committed to 'additionality', meaning that money from this source can't substitute for existing subsidy. Theatre people are in a quandary, since they want to use Lottery grants freely, yet don't wish to renounce the hard-won principle that government has a direct responsibility for the theatre. But can beggars be choosers? My suspicion is that, with the philosophies behind 'additionality' and Arts for Everyone already hard to reconcile, and the new administration keeping a tight rein on taxation and public spending, the Lottery cream will evolve into the sustaining drink itself.

Actually, the sums are pathetically small by most European standards. The average subsidy per seat in major German non-profit-making theatres, for instance, is over

£100, compared with less than £10 in Britain. In 1996–7 the English Arts Council and RABs spent about £50 million on the theatre, of which £20 million went to the National and RSC alone, and local authorities half that sum. Yet at the time of writing there seemed no sign of the increased core funding that the Labour government's fine words in opposition had seemed to promise.

So often politicians have defended subsidizing the theatre for reasons of national prestige, or because of its appeal to tourists, or because the 'cultural industries' are valuable. All that is true. Some 2.5 per cent of the British workforce is employed in the 'arts and culture economy'. Arts-related tourism is worth over £2 billion. The British Council estimates that exports from the 'cultural sector' are worth £10 billion. The turnover of VAT-registered traders designated as 'performers and performing groups' is well over £1 billion. The theatre is an important part of a major industry.

But it's the theatre's impact on the quality of life that justifies not only subsidy but the form's very existence. This was acknowledged by the Prime Minister Tony Blair when he became Leader of the Opposition in 1994. 'Theatre is not a luxury of economic progress,' he said. 'It is integral to our identity as a nation.' A thriving theatre 'helps us to understand life' and 'is central to the communities in which we live'. And in 1997 he suggested that the arts 'enrich the quality of our life', 'develop the creative potential of individuals', 'reflect society in new and imaginative ways' and help 'minds to open up and horizons broaden'. 'Through the arts we are able to enter the imagination of others', the Arts Minister, Mark Fisher, wrote the same year. 'They carry forward the values and beliefs of our past. They transform the way we see the world; they transform us.'

Though this represents a refreshing deepening of thinking, what does it bode in practice? Sadly little as far as Arts Council funding is concerned, but perhaps rather more for the Lottery. At the time of writing there were intimations that the nation's gambling profits might be used still more flexibly. Moreover, a Lottery-funded foundation, NESTA, should soon be investing in new creative talent and 'innovative' creative projects; schools will be required to produce regular 'arts statements', explaining the cultural opportunities they offer outside the classroom; there may be weekly pay-what-you-can nights at local theatres and an 'arts card', which will give school-leavers the same concessions at the box-office as students.

This should at least help ensure there are audiences for tomorrow's theatre. After all, how can I claim that technological advances will make live drama increasingly necessary if great numbers of people are never introduced to live drama? How can the social spread of audiences broaden unless people realise there are alternatives to TV and video? In America a presidential committee recently concluded that 'younger Americans are unlikely ever to attend live performances of musical and dramatic theatre.' The situation is less dire in Britain, but drama receives little emphasis in the curriculum and the evidence is that sixteen- to eighteen-year-olds in particular go seldom to the theatre. Somehow that must change.

Again, let's concede that the government isn't the sole begetter of new initiatives. For instance, the West End producers have introduced a plan under which costs are lowered in the smaller, less profitable theatres, making straight drama cheaper to stage. Moreover, the Arts Council hopes its 'venue development fund' will create a national network of small theatre spaces and encourage their owners to host adventurous work. That's particularly important, because small companies like Volcano or Frantic Assembly, roaming the land like gypsies, can be the most imaginatively exhilarating of all, and the 1990s have seen the demise of frighteningly many.

What will the pattern of British theatre be in 2010 or 2020? Will the current erosion have continued, meaning that if we're lucky we'll be left with two 'prestige' companies, a scattering of reps subsisting on co-productions with other theatres or with commercial producers looking for work to exploit, a Broadway-like West End, and a few unfunded companies permanently on the road? Or will Blair's idealistic rhetoric have actually turned out to mean something, permeating the political mainstream and releasing the funds to fill Eyre's 'stainless-steel kitchens', or indeed any cooking and eating space, with a diversity of food?

If I'm right to think that expensive technology will be more shunned than embraced by the theatre, the expense to the taxpayer or Lottery-player needn't be huge. But if government funding were closer to German or French levels, think of the possibilities! Parnassus Playhouse, Coketown, might afford to employ companies at a decent wage, cast more ambitious plays, tackle more adventurous work. We might get the spread of theatres of national quality in the British regions envisaged in the 1970s. Companies everywhere might again be able to take risks and even reclaim what was once called 'the right to fail'. The great foreign directors might more often bring their work to Britain, and the Brooks of the future not have to relocate in mainland Europe to find congenial conditions. Our own actors might find a career on the stage financially as well as artistically sufficient. Our dramatists might find it easier to resist the blandishments of film and television. We might be able to say that the British theatre is the best in the world without crossing our fingers behind our backs. The need will be there. The talent is already there. All that remains to be found is the political will.

Further Reading

Peter Brook, *The Empty Space* (1968)
Peter Brook, *There Are No Secrets* (1993)
Richard Eyre, *Utopia and Other Places* (1994)
Maria M. Delgado and Paul Heritage, editors, *In Contact with the Gods?: Directors Talk Theatre* (1996)
National Theatre Platform Paper 3, *Directors* (1992)
National Theatre Platform Paper 4, *Designers* (1993)
National Theatre Platform Paper 5, *Musicals* (1990)
National Theatre Platform Paper 8, *Playwrights* (1993)
Policy Studies Institute, *Culture as Commodity* (1995)
Arts Council of England, *The Policy for Drama of the English Arts Funding System* (1996)
The Arts Council Annual Report 1995–6 (1996)
Society of London Theatre, *Box-Office Data Report* 1995 (1996)
Barbara Isenberg, *Making it Big: The Diary of a Broadway Musical* (1996)
Augusto Boal, *The Theatre of the Oppressed* (1979)
Theodore Shank, *American Alternative Theatre* (1982)
George Steiner, *The University Festival Lecture for the University of Edinburgh* (1996)